17

A WRIGLEY BOOK
about
THE
MAGNET

BY DENIS WRIGLEY

This is a magnet.

A magnet pulls things to it,

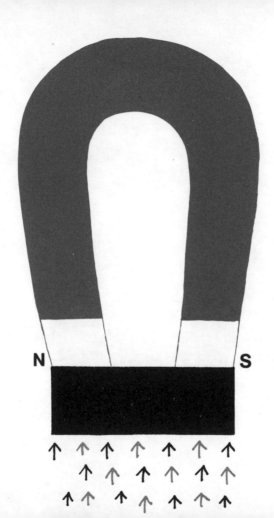

but not all things!

Only iron and steel
and some other metals.

Magnets can be of different shapes — bar or disc or horseshoe.

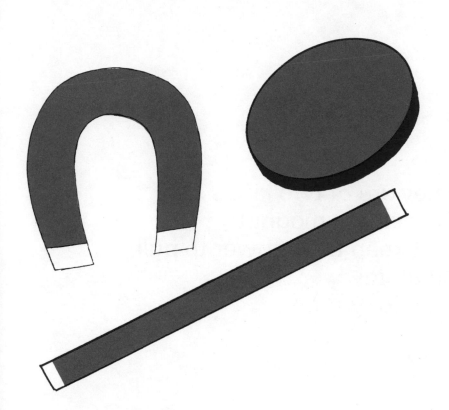

They are of two kinds . . .
Permanent magnets
that keep their power to pull
on metal
for a long time . . .

and electro-magnets,

which work as magnets
only when their connecting wires
are supplied
with electricity . . .

but stop pulling when
they are switched off!

The pull of a bar magnet is strongest towards its ends. Its ends are called North and South poles.

Poles which are alike push each
other away,
but poles which are not the same
attract each other.
A North pole pulls a South pole,
but pushes off another North pole.

The earth is like a big magnet.
It has a magnetic North pole
and a magnetic South pole.

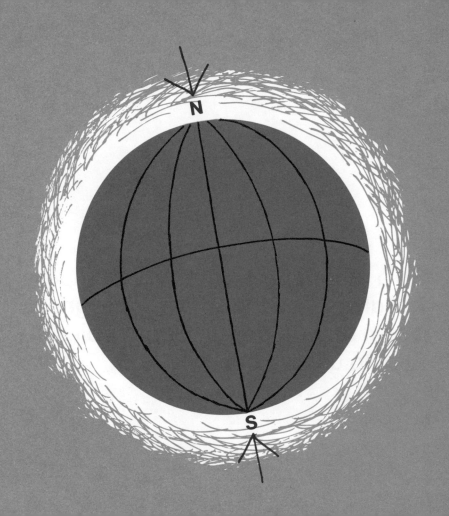

So a magnetic pointer in a compass will always swing towards magnetic North and magnetic South poles to help us find our way.

Magnets are used in telephones
to produce sounds,

and electro-magnets make bells ring
by pulling and letting go the clapper.

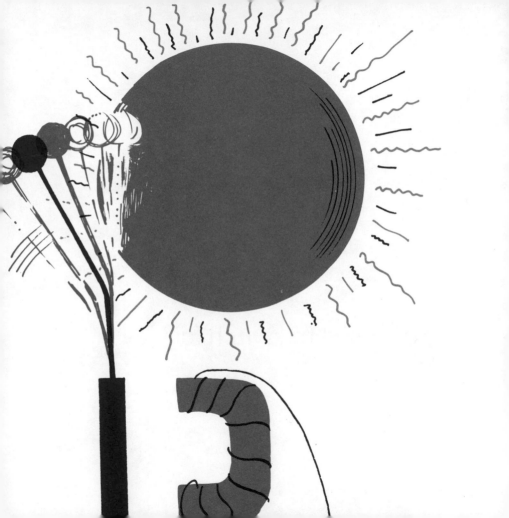

They are used to switch railway tracks . . .

and in electric clocks
and in microphones
and loudspeakers and tape recorders.

Magnets are used in play, too . . .

Look out for them!

First published 1978
Copyright © 1978 Denis Wrigley
ISBN 0 7188 2332 X
Printed in Hong Kong

The Wrigley Books

Published by
LUTTERWORTH PRESS • GUILDFORD AND LONDON